in his own words

Eric Clapton

Marc Roberty

OMNIBUS PRESS

LONDON · NEW YORK · PARIS · SYDNEY

Copyright © 1993 Omnibus Press
(A Division of Book Sales Limited)

Edited by Chris Charlesworth.
Cover & Book designed by Michael Bell Design.
Picture research by Virginia Lohle & David Brolan.

ISBN. 0.7119.3215.8
Order No. OP 47175

Exclusive distributors:
Book Sales Limited,
8/9 Frith Street,
London W1V 5TZ, UK.

Music Sales Corporation,
225 Park Avenue South,
New York, NY 10003, USA.

Music Sales Pty Ltd,
120 Rothschild Avenue,
Rosebery, NSW 2018, Australia.

To the Music Trade only:
Music Sales Limited,
8/9 Frith Street,
London W1V 5TZ, UK.

Photo credits:
The publishers are grateful to Virginia Lohle of STAR FILE, New York, and
the following photographers for their co-operation in the production of ths book:
Mickey Adair: 60 inset; De Bellis: 84; Dominick Conde: 49t; Dagmar: 28b, 37; Oliver Dzziggel: 13, 43;
Tony Gale: 16; Bob Gruen: 9, 32, 35, 36, 50t, 78r; Mike Guastella: 80, 89t; Steve Judson: 92;
Robert Knight: 90; Virginia Lohle: 46b, 47, 69x3; Jeffrey Mayer: 24t, 94; Phil Ollerenshaw: 67t, 76, 95;
Chuck Pulin: 10, 11, 12, 51, 55b, 58, 60, 65b, 66, 70, 74, 78tl; Phyllis Rosney: 93; David Seelig: 48,
54t&b, 56, 78bl; Andy Seghers: 52; Gene Shaw: 49b, 55t, 71, 71; Joe Sia: 30t, 41, 57;
Mike Wehrmann: 73b; Barrie Wentzell: 6, 29t&b, 30b, 31b, 34t&b, 53, 86;
Vinnie Zuffante: 45, 46t, 50b, 59, 65t, 79, 82, 83, 85t, 88, 96.
Star File pictures also appear on pages 14, 18, 20, 21, 22l&r, 25b.

   Additional photos: London Features International: 4, 7, 8, 19, 23t&b, 24b, 25t, 26, 27,
28t, 31t, 38, 39, 40, 42, 44, 61, 62, 63, 64t&b, 67b, 69br, 73t, 77, 85b, 89b, 91t&b.

Printed and bound in Great Britain by Scotprint Limited, Musselburgh, Scotland.
Every effort has been made to trace the copyright holders of the photographs in this book but one or
two were unreachable. We would be grateful if the photographers concerned would contact us.

A catalogue record for this book is available from the British Library.

Introduction

*My dedication to music has driven everyone away. I've had girlfriends but
I've ended up on my own. I used to find that lonesome image very attractive,
very bluesy, but now I'm stuck with it whether I like it or not...*

Eric Clapton has been a reluctant and rather parsimonious interviewee
for most of his long career. His quotes were short and to the point, and
he often gave the impression that he had little of interest to say and few
opinions to express. It sounds like a cliché, but he preferred to let his
music speak for him.

In recent years, however, he has opened up and shown himself
to be as erudite as many of his more loquacious contemporaries.
This may have something to do with his withdrawal from drugs and
alcohol... in the past, when reporters were around, he was probably
too befuddled most of the time to string together more than a few
quotable sentences. Compared to those days, he sounded like a
philosopher when Sue Lawley interviewed him on television during
early 1992.

It may also have something to do with his advancing years
and growing confidence in himself. For the guitarist they called 'God'
during the mid-Sixties was never happy with his elevation to deity,
and seems to have constantly but vainly sought subordinate roles
whenever possible in his subsequent career.

There is a mystique about Eric Clapton that he himself
has summed up as well as anyone in the quote above: material rewards
aside, he genuinely seems to have endured the life of the sorrowful
bluesmen, the musicians who inspired him to pick up the guitar in
the first place. Lost love, personal tragedy, drug dependency, loneliness
and insecurity have dogged him like a hellhound on his tail.

Nowadays he talks frankly about these aspects of his life, just
as he does about his musical past, his records, his peers and his lifestyle.
His own story, in his own words, is as eloquent as any biography.

Marc Roberty, September 1992.

Early Days, Inspiration and Influences

I grew up in Ripley, Surrey. It's about thirty miles outside of London, but it's very country - it's not even a town, it's a village with farms all around it. And very few people ever leave there. They usually stay, get jobs, get married.

I grew up listening to pop music first. Mostly songs that were still hanging around over from wartime, 'We'll Meet Again', that sort of thing, melodic pop music.

There was a funny Saturday-morning radio programme for children, with this strange person, Uncle Mac. He was a very old man with one leg and a strange little penchant for children. He'd play things like 'Mule Train', and then every week he'd slip in something like a Buddy Holly record or a Chuck Berry record. And the first blues I ever heard was on that programme; it was a song by Sonny Terry and Brownie McGhee, with Sonny Terry howling and playing the harmonica. It blew me away. I was ten or eleven.

The first guitar I saw was on TV. Jerry Lee Lewis was doing 'Great Balls Of Fire'. And that just threw me; it was like seeing someone from outer space. And I realised suddenly that here I was in this village that was never going to change, yet there on TV was something out of the future. And I wanted to go there! Actually, he didn't have a guitarist, but he had a bass player, playing a Fender Precision bass, and I said, "That's a guitar." I didn't know it was a bass guitar, I just knew it was a guitar, and again I thought, "That's the future. And that's what I want."

After that I started to build one, tried to carve a Stratocaster out of a block of wood, but I didn't know what to do when I got to the neck and frets and things.

I was living with my grandparents, who raised me, and since I was the only child in the family, they used to spoil me something terrible. So I badgered them until they bought me a plastic Elvis Presley guitar. Of course, it could never stay in tune, but I could put on a Gene Vincent record, look in the mirror and mime.

When I was fourteen or fifteen, they gave me a real guitar, an acoustic, but it was hard to play, I actually didn't even try for a while. And pretty soon the neck began to warp. But I did invent chords. I invented E and I invented A. I thought I had discovered something incredible. And then I put it down again, in my later teens, because I started to become interested in being an artist. The bohemian

Facing page: Eric in 1967, during his Cream period.

Above: Chuck Berry.

Right: Muddy Waters, Eric's adopted father.

existence beckoned more than the work. And at that point, when
I was sixteen, I started making weekend trips to London.

From hanging around in coffee bars and so on, I met a certain
crowd of people, some of whom played guitar. One was Long John
Baldry, who was then playing a twelve-string, doing folk blues.
Every Friday night, there would be a meeting at someone's house,
and people would turn up with the latest imported records from the
States. And shortly, someone showed up with that Chess album,
'The Best Of Muddy Waters', and something by Howlin' Wolf.
And that was it for me. For me it was very serious, what I heard.
And I began to realise that I could only listen to this music with people
who were equally serious about it.

I can get stimulated by new things, but to retap the root of what
I'm doing it for and what started me off, then I would need to go
back to an old record. The first thing I'd think of then would be
something like the Blind Willie Johnson album where the interview
is on one side and then him playing 'Nobody's Fault But Mine'.
That's probably the finest slide guitar playing you'll ever hear.
And to think he did it with a pen-knife, as well.

Otis Rush, Buddy Guy. It's not so much technique that I listen
for; it's the content, really, and the feeling and the tone.

Robert Johnson was so intense. It was difficult for me to take
in when I first heard the album 'King Of The Delta Blues Singers'.
A friend and I were both blues fanatics, and he was always ahead of
me in discovering things. We went through Blind Blake and

Blind Willie Johnson - working our way backwards, to the root of
it - and he finally came up with Robert Johnson. He played it for me,
and I couldn't take it. I thought it was really non-musical, very raw.
Then I went back to it, later, and got into it. First hearing it, it was
just too much anguish to take on.

     When I first got that Robert Johnson album, it had maybe
15 tracks on it, every one of them being completely dissimilar.
That's probably why I couldn't take it all in, in a way - it was too
much to cope with. When I did his songs, I would simplify huge
chord shapes that he would play with his fingers into one line and
make it easier. And when I did try to assimilate a style it came out of
the more recent Chicago soloists, like Freddie King - well no, he was
from Texas - but like BB King, you know, Buddy Guy. That was
more accessible to me than anything I heard by Johnson. It was almost
like Robert Johnson was too strong to mix with other people.
Too intense. Far too intense to be - to hang out, you know.
He was like a rebel in a way. I had all kinds of fantasies about him,
but that's what I pictured him as - as being a real lone wolf, who was
just too good for anyone to hang out with.

Below: Eric, Buddy Guy and Billy Joel at the
ELVIS Awards in New York, June 6, 1990.

Above: Eric and Buddy Guy jamming at
the ELVIS Awards.

I think he created a lot of the forms that became acceptable and
adaptable into rock'n'roll or simpler blues, more so than anyone else.
For instance, Blind Lemon Jefferson - I never took to him because it
never seemed that he would settle down. He was playing so many
figures around his singing all the time, it was difficult to relax or to get
a feel for his music. It was very - lots of filigree. And Robert Johnson
could accompany himself so simply that it was - it was evasive.
If you tried to pick it up, then you realised it wasn't simple. But it just
seemed - in a groove. And that would lay the pattern for generations
to come.

I think it's important for people to question music, ask where it came from. And what's amazing to me is that after 50 years later, generations of young musicians are still playing what he laid down without even knowing it, because they're getting it from my generation. And they think I invented it, or that I got it from Jimmy Reed or BB King or Howlin' Wolf, when in actual fact there's one guy in the back of it all really, in my way of thinking, that started maybe 10 different styles of playing blues - which are repeated, you know, rehashed over and over again today in very much the same way as he did it - completely on his own.

My background was a fairly disturbed childhood, because of an unusual family situation where I was raised by my grandparents under the illusion that they were my parents. And so, it was a kind of screwy set-up, which sorted itself out as I got older. But throughout my teens, I was very confused, angry and lonely. And that's what I got from listening to his music, much more than what I originally got from, say, Sonny Terry and Brownie McGhee, who had the instrumentation and the sounds of the blues, but were on the surface - well, when you get deeper into it - were actually more of an entertainment or an act. And most of the blues artists by the time I got to them were acts, you know. They were - not to put them down - slightly contrived. And were, a lot of them, playing to white audiences.
But Robert Johnson and that original record that I had - it ranks among all kinds of music. It's one of the strongest there is. And I wanted to be - I wanted to play like that, but it turns out that his life wasn't going to be that way for me.

I became a rock star. Even though it was against my will to begin with, that's the way it turned out. I enjoy it. Now, I mean I love the music, but it still sometimes annoys me that I didn't kind of...
Well, what could I have done? Even if I assimilated Robert's playing, I'd still be copying it.

In terms of playing I sometimes feel that spirit inside me when I play guitar or when I - even sometimes when I sing too. I don't know what it is. It's just - it's an embodiment of something that isn't necessarily an identity that he had, but just something that he expressed, which

Right: Carl Perkins and Eric at New York's Bottom Line, May 9, 1989.

Right: Eric at the ELVIS Awards.

I never heard anyone else do as well. And when I try to reach for that, whatever it is, it seems to come from the same place. I do identify with him and I keep seeing myself at a crossroads. Always going through that same sort of shift, where you come up to a situation and I don't know which way to go. I'm never, ever in a permanent situation. I'm never really satisfied with my lot, I'm always looking for something more. I'm directionless.

Freddie King was my first choice and I idolised him. I got the chance to play with him on tour - three tours together - and he was my support band! Can you imagine?! This was '75-'76, just before he died. He was a great guy to play with.

I can recall going back into his dressing room, and he would show me his gun and his knife, and then we would finish off a bottle of gin before he went on. The man was a hurricane, he was unbelievable, and there would always be a couple of spent women lying around!

And then he'd go on and play after this! I thought, "How can he? He's got the constitution of an ox!" He was big, and he made those ES335 Gibsons look like toys as he'd play with the strap on his right shoulder. A giant of a man.

He was my number one influence. He really was.

Initially I was very shy with Muddy (Waters); I was in awe. He was like the father of it all. And so whenever I was around him I tried to be as humble as possible and not start conversations, just let it come from him. As a result, I never pushed him in a researcher's way, I never asked him questions that I thought would be irritating. Like, I didn't want to ask him if he knew Robert Johnson. That to me would be a very disrespectful thing to do; a cold and distancing way of approaching it. So I talked to him the way a son would talk to his father, 'cause that's the way our relationship grew. I wanted a natural affection to develop, and I let it come from him. Gradually he would tell me things. He said his favourite song that I ever did was a Big Maceo song, 'Worried Life Blues', and that Big Maceo was one of his heroes.

I guess my fondest memory of him on stage was the last gig he ever did, which was to come with my show in 1983. He wasn't with the tour, he just turned up in Miami with his wife, and came on and did 'Blow Wind Blow'. That was a fantastic tribute and a great memory. The other great memory was me getting involved in a poker game with Muddy's drummer, 'Big Eyes' Willie Smith, and realising that I was being cheated which is often the situation. Muddy was going up and down in the halls, and I was in the room with the band, playing this dreadful game of poker, and watching my money disappear.

Muddy poked his head 'round the door and immediately sussed what was going on. He turned on this power and shut this guy down so hard - I've never seen anything like it - in a terrifying, loud voice. Oooo, man, it was scary. He went into dialect, and said things I didn't understand - at all. It was frightening, but I loved it.

I started out by playing folk-blues, things by Big Bill Broonzy and Ramblin' Jack Elliott, 'Railroad Bill', 'Cocaine'. But then I was drawn more and more toward electric blues, along with a few friends, a select few people. And, of course, then we had to be purists and seriously dislike other things. Then I went to art school.

Above: Eric, Albert Lee and Muddy Waters at the Sportatorium, Miami, June 30, 1982.

Art School and Early Bands

In 1961 Eric enrolled at Kingston-on-Thames Art College...

I was playing records most of the time, and getting drunk in the pub at lunchtime. I was an undesirable influence on the other students.

I used to draw men eating meat pies, for some reason, at the age of six. I don't know why. My grandparents were the first people to notice that I did have talent for perspective and things like this, which weren't taught to me. They were like gifts.

They encouraged me to go to art school, and I passed the necessary exams without any problems. I failed at English and maths and all other things, but I got through on the strength of painting and drawing.

At about the same time, unfortunately, I was seriously trying to play the guitar, and the one got the better of the other. I was actually thrown out of Kingston College of Art, because my portfolio at the end of the first year had nothing in it. Also, I think I went into the wrong department. There was Graphic Art and Fine Art, and I enrolled in Graphic, which meant that I was going to be a commercial artist. I should have been painting.

I still sketch now and then. I still use my eye as much as possible. That probably comes through in what I choose to wear, but nothing gives me pleasure as much as playing guitar. I still love to look at paintings, or even paint or draw, but it doesn't give me the high I get by playing in front of an audience. Nothing would.

During that time I met up with Tom McGuinness, who was going to get involved with a band, and I knew just about enough to be able to play and keep that end of it. So I got involved in that band, The Roosters, and that was a good feeling.

We (The Roosters) did 'Boom Boom' and a couple of other John Lee Hooker things, 'Hoochie Coochie Man' and some others by Muddy, I think. We did whatever we could get on records, really, on up to rock'n'roll things like 'Slow Down' by Larry Williams, because you had to have the odd rock'n'roll number in there.

Then Tom McGuinness brought in 'Hideaway' by Freddie King, and the B-side was 'I Love The Woman', which is still one of the greatest. And that's the first time I heard that electric-lead-guitar

Facing page: Yardbird Eric in Hyde Park, 1963.

style, with the bent notes - T-Bone Walker, BB King and
Freddie King, that style of playing.

Some of the band had day jobs that were more important to
them than the band. Practical considerations brought the band down.
But by that time, I had no other interests at all. I practised a lot.

After The Roosters, I got a job with Tom McGuinness in another
band, Casey Jones and The Engineers. That folded pretty soon, too,
and then I heard The Yardbirds had started up.

The Stones had been playing at the Crawdaddy Club, and when
they moved on, the next band in was The Yardbirds. I had met two
guys from The Yardbirds at some bohemian parties, and at that time
they were playing music by Django Reinhardt, 'Nuages' and so on.
We became friends. I went down to hear them at the Crawdaddy
and was fairly critical of them, especially the guitarist they had. I was
watching one week and playing next.

Playing with The Yardbirds put me in a very strange frame of mind.
I was all screwed up about my playing and I'd lost a lot of my original
values. I was really going to go off and paint or do something else.
I just didn't know.

My attitude within the group got really sour, and it was kind of
hinted that it would be better for me to leave. 'Cause they'd already
been to see Jeff Beck play, and at the time he was far more adaptable
than I was. I was withdrawing into myself, becoming intolerable, really
dogmatic.

Above: Eric and his Yardbirds colleagues
on The Serpentine, 1963.

Through The Yardbirds I was starting to feel very lost and alone. I was made to feel I was a freak, and started wondering if I was a freak. They all wanted the simple things of success and the charts, and what was wrong with that? "What's the matter with you? Why don't you want this?" And I began to think that I was really crazy.

I'll give you an idea of how different we were. I remember Paul Samwell-Smith arriving at rehearsal one day saying, "I heard a great record today." I said, "What's that, Paul?" "It's called 'The Elusive Butterfly Of Love'." Does that give you an idea of how different we were!

John (Mayall) called me up about two weeks after I'd left The Yardbirds. It suited me fine because it was a blues band and I was going through my purist number then. For me, in those days, blues was the only kind of music and I didn't like anything else.

They'd had a pretty big hit record 'Life Is Like A Slow Train Crawling Up A Hill' which actually caught on in America. I'd seen them on gigs too. I'd seen them at The Flamingo. I wasn't that keen on them because I never really thought John had a lot of control over his voice. He seemed to know what he wanted to do but not exactly how he wanted to do it. But, I mean, there were very few people around that could do anything properly. It was all very rough in those days, wasn't it? Except for maybe Georgie Fame who had what he was doing together, but most people were imitating other people pretty poorly.

Always after a little while you start to find things that you're slightly ashamed of being in a band for - I mean, just quirks. John has many quirks, believe me. Bands, when they've got a leader, often gang up against him behind his back and in The Bluesbreakers we used to really take the piss out of him behind his back on stage.

I used to live at John's house for a long time in a room that was like a cupboard. He was amazing, man. I mean, no one was allowed to drink! John McVie got slung out of the band wagon half-way between Birmingham and London one night because he was drunk and he had to make his own way home.

Also, he had his own bunk bed in the van did John, and you had to sit upright in the front while he got into bed in the back. And if we did a gig in Manchester where his parents lived, he'd go and stay the night at his mum's and we'd have to sleep in the van. He didn't get you a hotel or anything. So there were those disadvantages being in that band!

I was living in a place with some pretty mad people - great people, really. We were just drinking wine all day long and listening to jazz and blues, and we decided to pool our money, buy an estate car and take off round the world. The job with Mayall had become a job, and I wanted to go and have some fun as well. So we ended up in Greece,

playing blues, a couple of Rolling Stones songs, anything to get by.

We met this club proprietor who hired us to open for a Greek band that played Beatle songs. Then the Greek band was involved in a terrible road accident in which half of them were killed, and I found myself obliged to play with both bands. I was a quick learner then; I learned all the Beatles and Kinks songs they were doing, and I began to realise I was trapped, that the proprietor wouldn't let me go. He fired the rest of our band, and I was stuck there, with this Greek band. A couple of weeks of that, and I escaped somehow, headed back up here.

When I got back with John Mayall, Jack Bruce was on bass, and we hit it off really well. Then he left to go with Manfred Mann, and John got John McVie back. I decided that playing with Jack was more exciting. There was something creative there. Most of what we were doing with Mayall was imitating the records we got, but Jack had something else - he had no reverence for what we were doing, and so he was composing new parts as he went along playing. I literally had never heard that before, and it took me someplace else. I thought, well, if he could do that, and I could, and we could get a drummer... I could be Buddy Guy with a composing bass player. And that's how Cream came about.

Facing page: Eric with Cream on Ready Steady Go! in 1966.

Below: Cream: Eric, Ginger Baker and Jack Bruce, 1966.

Cream, 'Layla' and Beyond

Cream was originally meant to be a blues trio... sort of like Buddy Guy with a rhythm section. We were going to play small clubs... we didn't want to be big in any way. We had gigs when you could have mistaken us for Hendrix, it was so good... but on a bad night, uurggh.

Well, those guys (Cream) were pretty strong personalities. I hadn't taken that into consideration. At the first rehearsal, most of my ambition to lead the group went out the window, because I realised I didn't have the wherewithal. Whatsoever. I mean, when it came to forceful personalities Ginger was the man. And Jack was vying for the role. So I just let them get on with it, and backed off.

My way of introducing material I thought we should do was just play it. After the fights had died down at rehearsal I'd start playing a riff, and then one of them would go, "Aye, whot's zat?" I'd say, "Well, it's just something I'm kind of writing." "Aye, well, maybe we could do that."

Below: Cream on Ready Steady Go!, 1966.

It was very tense and hesitant stuff, a situation where I hadn't the confidence or the experience to stand up and dictate what we were going to do.

I think it was a sense of humour; it wouldn't allow us to be any particular thing. If it got too much into a straight rendition of anything, one of the members would have to sort of elevate it from just being repetitious or stereotyped. One ingredient would become parody, and then it would become something original. We were also very, very image-conscious. We were trying to do something totally original.

The lengthy guitar solos and improvisation may have been a stepping stone for a lot of the heavy metal things that happened. I always assumed that Zeppelin was the beginning of it. (1980)

In Cream there was a constant battle between Ginger and Jack. They loved one anothers' playing but they couldn't stand the sight of each other. I was the mediator and I was getting tired of that. Then Rolling Stone called me 'the master of the cliché' which just about knocked me cold. At that time, I decided I was going to leave Cream. Another interesting factor was that I'd heard the tapes from 'Music From Big Pink' by The Band and I thought... 'Well, this is what I want to play, not extended solos and maestro bullshit, but just good funky songs'. The Stone piece and 'Big Pink' convinced me I was going to pull out of Cream.

There have been rumours of a Cream re-formation...

Well, it's still a possibility, as long as we're all alive. But it hinges on how much people change, and how much they don't change. If we got back together, how far back would it go into the misery of what we experienced? Would that come back with it? It scares the living daylights out of me, because there was a lot of hostility, a lot of aggression and a lot of unpleasant personality clashes. But I was speaking to Robbie Robertson recently about Ginger Baker, and Robbie's had some great experiences working with Ginger. But we'd have to do it for love and out of the desire to have a good time. Not for the money.

I spoke to Ginger a couple of months ago, in fact. I mean, it's a bit like a marriage that you walked away from. Something about these people gets under your skin, and they're part of your life. (1988)

Cream was followed by Blind Faith, another ambitious 'Supergroup'...

Blind Faith was so short lived, we didn't ever really groove.
When we were rehearsing and hanging out before we ever toured,
we did a lot of great stuff.

I think Steve (Winwood) felt more unprepared for the over-
expectations that greeted us than I was. I wasn't that far out of Cream
when we started Blind Faith. It wasn't a big deal for me to go and
play for those kind of audiences. And I remember being concerned
about Steve's anxiety. When we started touring, what was wrong was
that we weren't ready. We weren't committed enough to each other
to survive it. (1975)

I think the 'Blind Faith' album is a lovely record. I like its looseness.
It's like a supersession record, except it's got a little something more
than that. You can feel there's a lot of longing in the band.

I wrote 'Presence Of The Lord' in C, which is pretty high
for me. Also, I was very overwhelmed by Steve's presence as a singer.
I don't think I could have stood out in the studio and sung it while he
was there. I was totally without confidence at the time as a singer.
That song was a true statement of what was happening in my life at
the time. I had somewhere to live. I was actually having a good
time after leaving Cream, feeling very secure. I was in a great frame
of mind.

That was just a song of gratitude. I'm not a religious person,
never have been. But I've always found it very easy to say thank you
to God, or whatever you choose to call him, for whatever happens,
which is nice to me. It's no problem for me to be grateful.

Right: Bonnie Bramlett, Delaney Bramlett
and Eric at London's Royal Albert Hall,
December 1, 1969.

Above: Eric (front, right) backstage at London's Lyceum with John Lennon, Yoko Ono, George Harrison, Keith Moon and others after the 'Peace For Christmas' concert, December 15, 1969.

In September 1969, Eric was invited by John Lennon to join his Plastic Ono Band for a one-off festival show in Toronto...

John (Lennon) gets these things. I mean, he just sits there and thinks up these things to do that you wouldn't believe. I just had a phone call on the day we were to leave and he said that someone had asked him to do that concert and it was that night!

So I had to make it to the airport in an hour, we went across on the plane and while we were flying he told me what he was going to do and he had a couple of songs like 'Cold Turkey' – I had to learn that, and just sort of generally rehearse on the plane. There weren't many people on it but it was still quite strange. Then we got off the plane and we were driven to the gig.

The gig was fucking good, yeh. I thought it was excellent because I'd played with him once before on The Stone's Circus thing but I hadn't a lot of experience of playing with John; it was a thing that paid off, a blind faith thing that paid off. I like the album, I thought it was very good and I don't think that he'd entertained the idea of solo performances before that. (1974)

Eric's next venture was his tour with Delaney and Bonnie, and his first solo album, titled simply 'Eric Clapton'...

After the Blind Faith tour, I lived with Delaney for a while and started talking about me making a solo album with his band. We started out with a tour of England and Europe, as Delaney and Bonnie and Friends with Eric Clapton. And having got me to sing, Delaney started trying to get me to compose, as well. So we were writing a lot. And that was great. He'd start something off, and when I came up with the next bit, he'd say, "Look what you can do." Some of the time I think it was so he could get fifty percent of the songwriting, but it was also inspiring me. By the end of that tour, I was ready to make the album and felt very sure of myself. (1988)

Right: Delaney and Eric at the
Royal Albert Hall, December 1969.

In a way it (the album) was a vehicle for Delaney's frustrations with himself. He may have been projecting himself on me a lot. And that comes across a lot on the record. I don't mind it at all. I enjoyed it and learned a lot in the process. He was prepared to be my coach, and no one had ever offered that to me before. He was the first person to instil in me a sense of purpose. And he was very serious about it. He was a very religious person, saying things like "You've got a gift. If you don't use it, God will take it away." It was quite frightening when I looked at it that way.

Delaney was an old friend of JJ Cale's. He played me the original version of 'After Midnight', which isn't dissimilar from the one on the 'Eric Clapton' record. It wasn't until later that I really became an appreciator of JJ.

This was followed by Derek And The Dominos, and the eponymous album which spawned 'Layla'...

We made our bones, really, on that album with George ('All Things Must Pass'), because we'd just got together and we were rehearsing and living at my house, and we had no gigs, there was no game plan at all. We were just living there, getting stoned, and playing and semi-writing songs.

When George said, "Can I use some of the guys?" I said, "Yeah, help yourself!"

"But," I added, "let's just make a deal. It'd be nice if we could get Phil Spector (George's producer) to produce something for the band." George said, "Okay, what we'll do is get Phil to produce an A- and B-side for you and your first single, and then we'll use the band for my album." (1984)

Tony Ashton (of Ashton, Gardiner & Dyke) suggested we call ourselves Del And The Dominos because he always used to call me Del. So it became Derek And The Dominos. It was last minute, in the dressing room before we went on stage at the Lyceum. We didn't have a name up to that point. You don't think of that when you're

forming a group. In fact, when someone suggests to you that you get a band title that's when you really start to worry about whether you should have a band at all, because you realise so much hinges on the name and you've blown the whole gig no matter what the music's like.

It wasn't a conscious attempt at anonymity. We presumed that everyone would know what it was all about. That it would be an open joke.

I had no idea what 'Layla' was going to be. It was just a ditty. When you get near to the end of it, that's when your enthusiasm starts building, and you know you've got something really powerful. You can be so-so as you're making the track, singing the vocals, but if as you start to add stuff and mix it, it becomes gross, then you really are in charge of something powerful. What I'm saying is, when I started to do that, it didn't feel like anything special to me. If you try to write something that's already got all of that, it's impossible. You just try to write something that's pleasing, and then try to get it to that.

I'm incredibly proud of 'Layla'. To have ownership of something that powerful is something I'll never be able to get used to. It still knocks me out when I play it. You know what? That riff is a direct lift from an Albert King song. And I don't have to pay royalties because... Hmmmm, maybe I do (laughs). It's a song off the 'Born Under A Bad Sign' album ('As The Years Go Passing By'). It goes 'There is nothing I can do/If you leave me here to cry'. It's a slow blues. We took that line and speeded it up.

But the funny thing was that once I'd got 'Layla' out of my system, I didn't want to do any more with The Dominos. I didn't want to play another note.

I went back home and stayed there and locked all the doors.

I feel like I'm compromising myself doing 'Layla' every night (1975 USA tour). I felt that way since we started doing it. You can't progress much with the format of that song. It's locked in there and you have to do it almost the same every night. It's sort of... disheartening in a way. As soon as we get that out of the way, we try and change everything around as much as we can. I still firmly believe in it, but you can only sing a song like that so many times before you run out of passion for it. (1975)

I suppose I often am tired of it. There'll be nights on this tour (1985 - Behind The Sun) when I'll be dreading doing it, because it can fall a little flat. If we play it really well, it's fun. But I have been playing it for the last fifteen years, so you can imagine that you have to work up a lot of false enthusiasm for something like that. If it works, it's great, but if it doesn't it leaves you with a sour taste. (1985)

In 1971 Eric, then a heroin addict, took part in George Harrison's Concert For Bangla Desh in New York...

George (Harrison) got me to do the concert. I got there a week in advance because they called for rehearsals to be a week in advance - 'The gig is on Saturday, please be there on Monday' sort of thing.

So I arranged by long-distance phone calls that there'd be something there for me because my heroin habit was going strong. So I fly over and there's nothing there and we can't score. There was no way we could score because the only thing people seem to take in New York is smack cut by ninety-five per cent, nothing or talcum powder, and so they have to shoot it up in order to get any buzz.

I wasn't into that. I didn't really want to go that far and so it was just a question of lying on this hotel bed going through agony with people going out trying to get stronger and stronger stuff each time. All of it was like talcum powder. So finally one of the cameramen came up with this medicine that he took for his ulcers which turned out to be a heroin substitute - Methadone. It got me straight enough so that I could go on stage and play. It was like the last day and on the day of the gig these guys got me the right thing to get me standing on stage, not looking too green, managing to know which way the audience was looking. I just managed it by the skin of my teeth otherwise I'd never got off the bed.

I think the tapes of the concert are fucking awful. I think I played so badly. It wasn't me at all. I just wasn't there. I wasn't there at all. (1974)

Above: Don Preston, George Harrison and Eric at George's Concert For Bangla Desh at New York's Madison Square Garden, August 1, 1971.

Below: Pete Townshend and Eric during Eric's 'Comeback' concert at London's Rainbow Theatre, January 13, 1973.

In 1973, after two years of self-imposed exile brought on by his addiction, Pete Townshend organised a coming out concert for Eric at London's Rainbow Theatre...

Pete (Townshend) is a mysterious person to me. I think he's great and I admire him, but I would never try and do a thesis on him. That's beyond me. I just don't know why he picked on me to do the Rainbow Concert. It could've been anybody but I'm grateful he chose me. I was just pleased to be doing it because I wouldn't have made up my mind to do it on my own. It had to be someone dragging me around by the scruff of my collar and making me do this and that.

I thought the gig was OK. I had a good time doing it. It was when I listened to the tapes afterwards that I realised that it was well under par. It was like a charity benefit in a way, you know. They got me out, got me on stage and tried to get me at it and I was being pushed more than I was pulling. I did it really because it was for Pete most of all. I wasn't really ready to go on stage. Although my

reluctance was great I really loved the feeling. The welcome
I got really moved me, it really did.

I think there were too many people on stage for the way it
was recorded. They recorded it on something like an eight track
and so they had to mix a lot of things together while they were
recording, which meant that the rhythm section suffered and you got
the bass and drums mixed in together. It was just not very satisfactory
in that aspect. I mean, it was very hard to mix.

The Rainbow Concert.

Above: Ronnie Wood, Eric, Ric Grech,
Pete Townshend.

Below: Eric and Pete.

Eric Clapton and his Band: the Tours and Albums

When I got out of that hibernation I thought, well fuck, look at the time I've wasted. I haven't really done anything with my life. Then suddenly I discovered this great hoard of cassettes which I'd forgotten all about but which I'd been doing all the time. Not many of them were actually usable songs but a lot of them were incredible performances. It's like I'd sit down and play a blues with just a guitar and when I played it back I thought, who the fuck is that? Sounds good! So I was blaming myself for not keeping my hand in when in actual fact I was still playing and singing as much as any other time.

I considered re-forming Derek And The Dominos before this band got together. I was saying "Who am I going to play with? I don't want to look in the Musicians' Union book and look up the most famous names." I considered calling them all up but it never reached the stage where I picked up the phone. I just sat and brooded on it. And actually what happened was, Carl (Radle) sent me a telegram and said he had a band for me and did I want to play with them? So I brooded on that for a while and finally fell into it.

Going out on my own was a massive step, which really shook me. Because then I had to come to terms with the fact that I was also regarded as a pop musician, as well as a rock'n'roll musician, as well as a blues musician. So I had to present, and contrive in some way, an image that suited all of these categories without disowning any part of my audience. My ego wants to please all these areas. At first, I actually went on stage starting with an acoustic set - did three or four songs with a Martin - and then got into some rock'n'roll and a few blues. All the Seventies were like that in one way or another - trying to find my way. Later, I went through a period of thinking maybe I'd just do blues and R&B all night. But you can't ever satisfy everybody, or even yourself. Because if you do all blues, then you'd like to do 'Let It Rain' or 'Badge' because they're lighter and fun to play.

    For most of the Seventies I was content to lay back and do what I had to do with the least amount of effort. I was grateful to be alive. I didn't want to push it.

I was also tired of gymnastic guitar playing. And not only was
I tired of it in myself, it seemed the advent of Cream and Led Zeppelin
had woken up a whole spectre of guitar players who just wanted to
burn themselves into infinity. The more I heard about that, the more
I wanted to back off. I started to identify with like-minded people
like JJ Cale. When I listened to JJ Cale records, I was impressed by the
subtlety, by what wasn't being played.

Below: Eric and his band in
Copenhagen, 1974.

In 1974, this band released '461 Ocean Boulevard'...

I really had no ideas for '461' before I went to Miami. I just jammed and put it together as I went along. I played everything I could think of. I must have gone through a hundred songs. But I was frightened to expose myself to too much by bringing out the stuff I had written on my own during the three years before. I didn't really know anyone in the band. So we all just wrote there, or made things up. I left the tapes with Tom Dowd and said, "Pick out what you think is best and put it on the album."

George Terry played me the 'Burnin'' album, by Bob Marley And The Wailers, that had 'I Shot The Sheriff' on it. It took me a while to get into it. I was coming from a completely different place. To break my inherent musical tightness down into this real loose thing was very, very difficult for me to assimilate.

The 'Sheriff' track was conceived in Miami, with a Tulsa band. It was such a weird melting pot. The only way I could stamp my personality onto it was to sing it, and just play the occasional lick. The rest of it was almost out of control. It was a complete hybrid.

The record came out, and went up the charts, and shortly after that I got a phone call from Bob Marley. I don't remember where I was, or exactly what the circumstances were, but we had a half-an-hour conversation on the phone. And I kept asking him if it was a true story - did he really shoot the sheriff?? What was it all about?

He wouldn't really commit himself. He said some parts of it were true, but he wasn't gonna say which parts. The next time I spoke to him, he came to England with The Wailers and did a small tour - until one of them got sick with 'flu. None of them had ever had the

Right: Todd Rundgren and Eric at Madison Square Garden, New York, 1974.

'flu before. They thought he had a serious disease. They cancelled the tour and went home, 'cause it was cold then in England.
But I went to see them at the Hammersmith Odeon, and I walked into the dressing room that I couldn't see the other side of because of the smoke. I sat and talked to Bob, and he was just a great guy. He was so warm. A beautiful man. This was our first face-to-face meeting. (1988)

'There's One In Every Crowd' was released in 1975...

We were recording mainly with producer Tom Dowd then, and Tom's chief thing is that you should tap the source. If we wanted to play reggae, or we were being intrigued by reggae through Bob Marley, why not go to where it comes from?

Tom got us there for 'There's One In Every Crowd', which was almost 50-50 reggae stuff and Marcy Levy songs. When we got there, people were just wandering in and out of the studio, lighting up these massive trumpet joints. After a while, I didn't know who was in the studio and who wasn't, there was so much smoke in the room.

And Peter (Tosh) was weird. He would just be sitting in a chair - asleep, or comatose. And then someone would count it off and he'd wake up and play, with that weird wah-wah reggae chop. And then at the end of the take he'd just nod off again!

He didn't seem to know what the tune was, or it didn't matter. But then we'd get him to sing. He sang the pilot vocal to 'Burial', and also to 'Whatcha Gonna Do'. I couldn't understand a word.

I literally couldn't! It was hard enough when those guys talked because you'd have to ask, "Could you say that again slowly please." But when they sang, it almost completely disappeared. Even today, I don't know if I sang the right words on that! I have no idea. And if I did, I don't know what half of them mean.

We didn't release those two tracks because the feeling was that it was getting to be too much of a reggae thing. We'd just had a big hit with 'I Shot The Sheriff' and it was starting to become an over-powering influence. And there was a feeling of discontent amongst the band, too, that we were going off too much on a sidetrack. 'Cause when we got onto the concert stage we weren't going to be a reggae band, so the album had to reflect what we were going to do live. (1988)

'EC Was Here', a live album, also came out in 1975...

I didn't really want to put it out now, but the record company was worried about the sales of 'There's One In Every Crowd'. They thought if they put out a live record to coincide with a tour, that it would sell. I don't really understand their thinking, but I went along with them. I picked out the best tracks we had around. If there's any concept, it's an accident. (1975)

Above: Jimmy Page and Eric at the ARMS concert for Multiple Sclerosis, Royal Albert Hall, 1983.

... following a lengthy US tour...

It takes a long time to get your chops, you know. It really does. And the band was still trying to get to know one another, so I suppose I was underplaying a lot. I mean, I'm still not keen to project myself as a guitarist, 'cause there's too many others who can top me. There's always someone faster, isn't there? It's best to just try and play... well. Not necessarily brilliant.

From playing with him on this tour, I know that Carlos Santana is a very, very strong player. He really kept me on my toes. Basically, though, I don't like to give a specific opinion on someone else's playing. Not only is it unfair to another musician, but I'm not a competitive guitarist. I've settled into my own pace. If I have to change my ways in order to top a poll somewhere, I'd rather not play. (1975)

'No Reason To Cry' was released in 1976...

Woody (Ronnie Wood) came to stay with us in Nassau. He was pushing me around trying to get me to write songs but I couldn't because the situation was too idyllic. We finally wrote a couple of songs that we didn't use. One was called 'You're Too Good To Die You Should Be Buried Alive'. Can you believe that?!

After a couple of days I was walkin' 'round the studio (Shangri-La) saying "I'm packing it in, I don't want any more to do with it."

If I go in the studio with my band they're gonna look to me for something and I had nothing. Richard Manuel came up with 'Beautiful Thing' and from there we just went!

Dylan can't restrict himself to one way of doing a song so we did 'Sign Language' three ways. I thought fuck it, I'll just go loose as he is. I'm used to doing one song one way but Dylan throws caution to the wind every time.

He came down to the studio and we were trying to work and he goes in there and swans around for a little while in a black leather suit he's just got, and he managed to steal my percussionist's chick, who had one leg in a cast because she'd broken it. Not only that, but he stole all the clothes off Woody's bed, took the chick out through the window and shagged her in the tent in the garden outside the studio he had there ready for the occasion. With a cast on her leg! Outrageous fellow! (1976)

Below: Ronnie Wood, Andy Fairweather-Low and Eric at the ARMS concert in New York, 1983.

On August 5, 1976, at Birmingham Odeon, Eric, worse the wear for drink, apparently spoke out in favour of Enoch Powell...

I was drunk, and a drunk will blab off about anything to as many people as he can; you cannot believe anything a drunk says. The funny thing is that I was able to play through all that. The old survivor, the automatic pilot, still managed to help me play. But there were many occasions around that time when I had to be led offstage and given some black coffee or some oxygen. (1976)

'Slowhand' was released in 1977...

'Slowhand' for me is a very nervous sung album, especially after 'No Reason To Cry'. Maybe it was because of the lack of material we had when we went in to cut it, or the difference in surroundings.

And laid back is not the word for it! 'Layla' wasn't a success, it died a death, but as far as I was concerned, I'd have put that album up against anybody's that was out at the time. With 'Slowhand' it was a completely different story. It was lightweight, really lightweight, and the reason for that, I think, is partly due to the fact that some of the stuff that we wanted to put on the record I wrote, say, six months before.

We were on the road and we wrote some songs and got to the studio - and we couldn't get the studio early enough or we wanted a couple of weeks off or something like that - and by the time we got in there everyone knew the song so well, we were so sort of limp about it that it was lazy.

Anyway, for me, I think the best track has got to be 'Wonderful Tonight', because the song is nice. It was written about my sweetheart, and whether or not it was recorded well or we played it well doesn't make any difference, because the song is still nice.

Every now and then you fall in love again, albeit with the same woman, just one night for some reason - something she's said or the way she's approached the situation, and bang! you're in love again, and it's such a strong feeling you can't do anything else but write it down. (1979)

... followed by 'Backless' in 1978...

The title came from the Dylan gig we did at Blackbushe, where it became very apparent that he knew exactly what was going on everywhere around him all the time. So it's a tribute to Bob, really. I mean, if you were backstage, he expected you to be putting as much into it as he was. You couldn't just stand there and be one of the roadies, you had to actually focus all your attention on him, and if you didn't, he knew it, and he'd look at you and you'd get daggers.

I used to think the way to record an album was top what
you'd done before, but it doesn't work. It never works, because what
you've done before is in the past, and that's it. If you try and emulate
what you've done before, then you're in a rut, and you might as well
wave goodbye to the future altogether. So I didn't try.

The best things that happened on 'Backless' were the things
that happened at the time. I got away with one song on there,
'Golden Ring', which I think is the strongest song on the album,
because I wrote it because I was fed up with the general sort of apathy
of everyone involved, and I just thought, "Well, I'll take a song in
there and whether they like it or not, we'll do it - they'll learn it and
record it and we'll put it on the record, and that's that!" And that
kind of conviction carried the thing through. I spoke to Don Williams
just before Christmas and I told him I liked his album and he said
'Golden Ring' was his favourite track too, because it was the only one
that came through with any kind of feeling, with strength. And if
you listen to it, there's virtually nothing to it.

Songs like that are caused by situations, but situations of that
extremity don't happen every day, thank God, though if they did
I'd be the most prolific songwriter in the world. They only happen
once every two or three months, but there you go. That's why a song
is moving, because you don't think what the diction is like or how
clever the words should be or how well they should rhyme, it's just
like you're saying something to somebody, as if you're in conversation
with them.

I like listening to story type songs, parable type things with
a moral, but the songs that always hit me most are the ones where
I actually recognise what the guy is talking about, and it's as if he's
talking to me or talking to someone that I know or something like
that. It's like a conversation coming out of the record player.

Being critical of your own work is very difficult, especially
when you can just say 'Bow Wow' instead. In the case of 'Backless'
I think we were very lazy. In fact, I think all musicians are lazy.
I think that's one of the best parts about us. The trouble with being
lazy is you either don't try hard enough or you try too hard - and
you don't like being told what to do. But it does have its redeeming
points.

What is hard for me on this side of the argument is that I
live in England and my band lives in America, and we don't get to
groove enough. When we do it's usually somewhere where we can't
be interrupted. But that's cool, it's all right. (1979)

Eric's 'Tulsa Band' disbanded after his
US tour in the summer of 1979...

Toward the end of that particular band, we were gettin' out of
it again, and I was the lead. I started to get straight, but I was drinking
maybe two bottles a day of whatever I could get my hands on.
And there was real bad tension in the band that was aimed at me.
Then I hired Albert Lee. We became friends, and there was a division
between these two Englishmen and the Tulsa boys. And at the end
of this particular tour, I think it was in '78, I fired everybody.
Not only that, I didn't even tell them - I fired them by telegram.

Above: Eric and manager Roger Forrester.

And I never saw Carl again. He'd saved me at one point, sending me that tape, and I turned my back on him. And Carl died. It was, I think, drugs, but I hold myself responsible for a lot of that. And I have to live with that. (1984)

'Just One Night', a double live LP, was released in 1980...

I didn't really want to record it. There's a natural shyness about me when I'm playing on stage; for me it's something that should only happen once, you know, and then it's gone.

The album was one show. We did it two nights, and recorded both. I think they chose the one I didn't like. (1980)

... and there was a three year gap before 'Money And Cigarettes' in 1983...

I started working on that album with the English rhythm section, but I couldn't get any kick out of them for some reason. The thrill was gone, and there was a feeling of paranoia in the studio because they sensed it, too. I spoke to Tom Dowd about it, and he said, "Just be brutal. Fire them all, send them all home. They'll understand. And then we'll bring in some people." He brought in (bassist Donald) "Duck" Dunn and drummer Roger Hawkins, and the first day they came in, we set up and played 'Crosscut Saw' all day.

I found I was really getting stretched, and it was the first time I'd been stretched for several years, simply because I'd been playing with people who were laying back, and the more I laid back, the more they laid back. Whereas this rhythm section, they counted themselves off and started playing, and I didn't have to be there. If I wanted to get in on it, I had to work fucking hard. And that's when I decided I was getting back to where I should be. (1984)

Eric took part in the ARMS Charity Concerts, inspired by Ronnie Lane's multiple sclerosis, with an all-star cast...

At the shows, there was no doubt that everyone in the audience got a great deal out of seeing all these strange people together. It was like a circus, though I don't think it always has to be that way. In that particular situation, it needed Ronnie (Lane) to be in great pain and need help, in order to pull it together. That kind of show always needs an impetus, some kind of motivation that breaks down the ego barrier. If you put something like that together for its own sake, it could be a nightmare, because of the arguments that would ensue, the egos involved. Of course, Ronnie and I have been friends, blood brothers, in fact, for years. (1984)

He also joined former Pink Floyd mainman Roger Waters' touring band on his The Pros And Cons Of Hitch Hiking tour...

I've never come across music like that, or had to play that way before in my life. It really was off the beaten track for me. That gig was like playing John Cage or Stockhausen - wearing headphones with click tracks going on, being ready for cues, and things like that.

I like to have the time where I can get away from being in the lead. It's like having a little holiday in a way. It gives you a sense of reality. If you lead your own band and you do a lot of promotion work and interviews yourself, you become wrapped up in yourself too much. And my ego tends to fly off the handle too easily. I get wrapped up in believing that what I do is faultless and I walk down the street and say, "Hey, everyone feel alright? I'm feeling great." So when you work with someone else you really have to learn how to slot in a band and make it sound good. (1985)

Above: Eric on stage during Roger Waters' Pros And Cons Of Hitch Hiking tour, 1984.

Above: Eric and Phil Collins, 1985.

Below: Phil Collins and Nathan East.

'Behind The Sun' was released in 1985...

I wasn't very aware of Genesis; I didn't have any of their records, and wasn't too sure what they were like. It wasn't until I got to know Phil (Collins) that I realised what a good drummer he was and that his tastes in music were akin to mine - the fact that we both like black music the best. I heard the way he was producing John Martyn, and I heard Phil's own things, and I thought I would like to have him produce my record. He's got a great understanding of synthesizers and how they can be used without becoming overpowering.

We were going more for atmosphere than for a sound, something intangible. Also it was a working relationship that was very creative. I knew it would be easy, from having been around him when he's been making records. We get on very well in the studio; it's a great relationship.

The title track ('Behind The Sun') was done at Phil's house, in one take on an eight-track. That's the kind of thing I do when I'm working on little tape machines. I do lots of things like that but never thought of putting them on a record, because I don't think record companies would accept it. I think they only accepted it in this case because it was so short and we snuck it on the end of the album.

Phil and I made the record, finished it, mixed it and sent it off, and thought no more about it. I should say that we made the record on Phil's wish and my wish too. We wanted the record to be the first album to be a true portrayal of what I could do in all the areas that I play in: there was a little reggae, a little acoustic blues, and a lot more of my playing that Roland (guitar synthesizer), sounding like a saxophone, a harmonic and so forth. We were very satisfied with it as a concept album, you know, showing the different sides of me.

Well, Phil went on to his next project and I was doing some film music and that was the end of that. Then we got this message from Warner Bros saying that the record wasn't strong enough. I asked why, and they said because it needed more songs that would be able to be taken off as potential hit singles. I was very upset of course, because I'd never considered that to be a priority in my life, and still don't. But, I suppose I had to bend with it and I wanted to know from them what they thought hit single material was. So they sent me some songs by Texas songwriter Jerry Lynn Williams, which I liked a great deal. I said yeah, sure, I'll do them, and we'll see how it works out. But I think it would be best if you produced them, I told them. Phil couldn't do it; he was already locked into something else. I thought it would be best if Warners produced the songs, and provided the musicians. So if any mistakes were made it would be in their camp; it was kind of a tactical game, you know. So I went back to America and did those songs in Los Angeles with what they call the A-team (Jeff Porcaro, Steve Lukather, Michael Omartin and Greg Phillinganes). (1988)

Above: Nathan East, Eric, Greg Phillinganes and Phil Collins at the Royal Albert Hall, 1989.

A track from 'Behind The Sun' - 'Forever Man' - involved Eric in his first video...

It was fun, but it goes against the grain for me. It's a concession to the starmaking machinery. I've always found the video thing a bit obnoxious. Funnily enough, when I was young I used to love to track down rare footage of Jerry Lee Lewis, Chuck Berry and people like that. I would have given my right arm to see that stuff. But now you're swamped with it, it's the other extreme. There's something a bit tasteless and gross about the whole thing for me. The mystery is being taken out of the music. Just turn on the TV and everyone's there, ramming themselves down your throat - ah, I don't know, it makes me sad. Music for me has always been something to close your eyes to, to have your own picture.

'August' was released in 1986...

Whenever I make a record my life seems to change yet again. The nature of that depends as much on the influence of the people

Facing page: Robert Cray and Eric at Madison Square Garden, New York, April 27, 1987.

Above: Steve Ferrone, Eric and Nathan East;

Right: Eric and Keith Richards at The Ritz, New York, November 23, 1986.

involved as it does upon the music. It's as if, like a sponge,
I absorb the general vibe and the change slowly starts to take place,
new patterns of thought, new forms of language, new musical
directions, new things to laugh at, and then suddenly it's all over and
we have to say goodbye until the next time.

I think I sold myself a long time ago. I made some kind of
deal with myself to get along, to please people, just make life easy,
I think. It disturbs me a little to hear myself say that but I have to
admit it because otherwise who am I kidding?

When the Warner Brothers thing came up I suddenly
realised that the Peter Pan thing was over. Because just before that
Van Morrison had been dropped - mightily dropped - and it rang
throughout the industry. I thought, if they can drop him they can
drop me. There was my mortality staring me in the face. (1986)

... followed by 'Journeyman' in 1989...

I wanted to get Jerry Williams in and the Womacks, because
I thought it would be interesting to see how we would marry in the
studio. If it would work. It was just an experiment, really, and with
the Womacks it worked incredibly well. With Jerry it worked, but
we had to confine Jerry, really, to a rhythm part, because he's a wild
man. Two years ago I would have been completely submerged by
him. My personality up until quite recently would have quite
happily stepped aside and let him take the lead role. This time it
didn't happen. I was very firm in making sure this record was for me,
that I was going to be singing it and that you were going to be
accompanying me if you were in the studio. And with someone as
strong as Jerry's personality, that's no mean feat.

   We played 'Hound Dog' because Russ (Titelman, the producer)
thought it would be a good vehicle for me. And I was like, "Oh,
I don't really know about that, but I'll do it because you think it's a
good idea." And then I thought, "Well, let's do 'Before You Accuse
Me'," because I'd always liked the Bo Diddley version. So we tried to
do it like that. But 'Old Love', well, that I wrote with Robert Cray.
We'd done these two things, and we had a week of time together.
And it was like, "We've got to do something." So I started playing
the first part of the progression, which is A minor to F to G suspended
to G, and then Robert started playing along with me. This was one
of those intervals in the studio where no one's doing anything,
everyone's kind of lost the thread, and we just started playing this.
Robert came up with the turn-around at the end, and then I started
writing the words. He wrote 50 percent of the words, and we just
did it. It was a perfect collaboration. He took 50 percent of the guitar
playing. I took 50 percent. The only thing we didn't share was
singing. I wanted to keep that for me. I thought that was one of the
best marriages on record that I've done. I think the feeling after we'd
done it was, "Well, we've got it. We've got what we came in
here for." (1989)

Top left: Keith Richards and Eric at the
ELVIS Awards, New York, May 31 1989.

A lot of people have said to me that their favourite track on the album is 'Hard Times'. That really shook me, because I didn't think they would like that. I thought that was almost too ancient in a way, in its approach, for anyone to like it. But there are people out there that want that. And it's very encouraging for me to know that I can make an album in six months' time, or maybe more, that will be comprised of entirely that kind of thing.

Each year since 1987 Eric has performed a series of shows at London's Royal Albert Hall...

Yeah, well, we recorded my shows at the Albert Hall this year and the year before, and we've amalgamated it to make a live record, which is... well, some of it is superb, and some of it isn't superb. It's good, but... I'm very critical of my own performance. I tend to think when I walk offstage that it was brilliant, and then when I listen back to it, I'm not that satisfied. I never am.

It's a selfish thrill to play with an orchestra. But it hasn't
really clicked. It's a very hit-or-miss process, because they play in a
different time scale. They hit the beat just slightly after the conductor's
baton comes down; they play behind the beat, in effect. I play right
on the beat or sometimes in front of it. I like pushing the beat, and
so the marriage is very difficult. It's a challenge to get it right.
But more often than not, it's a very painful disappointment. But it
is a great sound live, to hear all that moving air coming from violas
and cellos, double basses and fiddles. And to have an electric guitar in
the middle of that, quite hard, it's a tremendous feeling. (1991)

Cream's farewell concert was there and I always liked it.
You come off stage at the end of your last gig at Wembley and you
don't ever want to go back on there. Whereas the Albert Hall had
this promise of some kind. It seemed you could do different things
in there.

It has a very scholastic setting. But last year the boxes were
full of executives bringing their clients to show off and a lot of the
time they were having little parties in there, getting pissed with their
backs to the stage. It's a difficult situation. This ticket thing has not
worked to everyone's satisfaction. We've had a lot of complaints.
They're gone quickly and a lot of times it's to the wrong people.
Many of the audience seem to be looking for a cosy evening out.
They don't want too much demanded of them. You can tell by the
odd request that gets shouted up that they want to live in the past.
It would be difficult at the Albert Hall to do more than three new
songs and expect them to go down well.

Above: Cream's Farewell Concert,
Royal Albert Hall, November 26, 1968.

When things are going well that's great. Last year I came off stage after what I thought was a really good gig and there was a buzz backstage. It seems that someone had been caught getting a blow job and asked to leave. In the stalls. Not in a box. Out in the wide open spaces.

I'm a very habitual person, and I like nothing more in my life than to have a routine, even if it's only a yearly project at the Royal Albert Hall. I don't see any reason for it to end. To me it's like setting up a new proms. Because, yes, I do tend towards delusions of grandeur. It's a failing of most musicians I find. And next year's had to be a mammoth production. It started after the nine shows we did there last year when I said to Michael Kamen, who worked on the scores of Edge Of Darkness and Lethal Weapon 2, "Would you write me a concerto?" I thought it would be nice to have a concerto, not just for guitar, but for my guitar, composed around the way I play. It's up to me to write the second movement. Are you familiar with the Rodrigues guitar concerto? Well, you must have heard the second movement, that's where all the heavy melodies are. It's very slow and passionate.

'Unplugged', an album of acoustic versions of Eric's best known songs was released in 1992...

There's not much I can say about these songs, except that they helped me through a very, very hard patch in my life. (1992)

Right: Steve Cropper, Eric and
Bob Dylan at the Dylan Tribute Show at
Madison Square Garden, October 16, 1992.

The Blues Versus Commercialism: Songwriting and Confidence

I don't think blues ever goes away. But I don't think you'll
ever see a real resurgence of it. It's always just going to be there.
More than any style of music, because no matter what direction rock
music goes in, it has to stay with the blues. That's the spine and
body of it.

It's so much to do with fashion as well. When they started
showing those Levis 501 ads on TV, people were hearing Sam
Cooke and Ben E King for the first time. To those ears, they were
brand new names. And it is a shock to me now that people have never
heard of Otis Redding for instance. Never heard of James Brown.
So when people become reborn through commercials or whatever
it is - through jean adverts, it doesn't matter really. But it's still quite
a shock to me, because when I listen to music, I've got a very curious
mind. I want to know where it comes from, what preceded it. And it
shocks me when people buy singles or albums without ever having
that investigative nature. (1988)

Because of the identity crisis of having to like what you do
as much as what you've liked in other people, your role models or
your heroes, having to put it in the market place alongside what
they've done. One of the things I remember Tom Dowd or Ahmet
Ertegun saying to me: "Don't forget, when you sell a record, you're
selling alongside Frank Sinatra and BB King and Quincy Jones,
people of that stature. And you've got to think of yourself as one of
them. And when you do, when you can make that comparison and
be comfortable with it, you'll have got somewhere." That's the
way I'm starting to think. It's taken me a long time. I'm a slow
learner, and a slow developer. And no doubt drink and drugs were
instrumental in keeping me from that growth. But it's taken place
now. Maybe too late - not too late, I don't think. But late for sure.
But I've come to terms with my identity a lot better.

It's important for records to be as good as you can make them.
You know? When I've written songs and made them into demos -
for instance, on the 'August' album I had one demo which we

Above: Steve Cropper, Eric, Bob Dylan and
Tom Petty at the Dylan Tribute Show.

did clean up and polish a lot. Which I could never play in concert
because it never reached that level of the demo. And another one
that's called 'Tearing Us Apart', which I do do in concert and which
is exactly the same as the demo. It varies according to how much of
myself has come through. 'Tearing Us Apart' - that is purely me.
There's no façade in that. But I don't write that much to really qualify
me being that up front about it. So, for instance, in Jerry Williams'
case, I tend to think his material is so malleable, it's so easily
adjusted, that I can put myself into that and be really me, singing
his words with his chord changes. I don't feel that I'm hiding behind
him in any way.

It's just that certain songs that he writes are the kind of things
that I would like to write but I don't get around to.

I tend to think - not in a malicious way - that I used people
like Ben Palmer, Delaney or Jerry Williams, to convey what I was
feeling without me having to do the leg work. Because of my lack of
belief in myself. I think I was aware of it, but my excuse was that I
was taking something from them, yes, but I was giving them the
ability to be known, the possibility for the audience to know them.
The reason for instance, why I joined Delaney's band was because
I was in total awe of him, and I thought everyone else should see this.
I knew that I had the drawing power, even then. I could make the
public aware of them just by putting my name on the bill. And I still
use that a lot.

I think it's a combination of things that have gone back to when I was first adulated, where I was put in a position of pressure that whatever I would write or play wouldn't be as good as I would like it to be. That has been something I've had to bear with over all these years. Something that has taken a long time to come to terms with. To the point now, to give you an example, I walked on stage with Elton John on Saturday night without one reservation. Now two years ago, or even a year ago, it would have been a lot harder to deal with. And I would say yes at the outset, and then sat in the audience and just thought about that moment when I was going to have to walk on stage. Now I sat and enjoyed the show, and at the time when I was supposed to get up, someone came and told me, and I walked up and played, and it was just like water off a duck's back. I really enjoyed it, and I had no idea what I was going to play, I just knew I was going to be me. And whatever came out would be me. Didn't know the song. Didn't know the changes. But felt no fear whatsoever. And that to me is a miracle. I've got to that point now, and it can only get better - I hope.

I read in Laurence Olivier's autobiography where he got stage fright at the age of 57. And for a year suffered from the fact that he couldn't remember lines. Every night. So that can always happen.

But at this moment in time I'm pretty comfortable with what I can do. I know my limitations, really. And try to push them - but I stay within them, too.

Below: Ringo Starr, Elton John, Eric, Jeff Lynne and George Harrison during the Prince's Trust Concert, Wembley Arena, June 1987.

Guitars, Playing and Equipment

My first guitar was a cutaway Kay electric, and very expensive at the time. And a bitch to play. Had a big thick neck, and very high action which you couldn't lower without touching the fret bars. It was very heavy and unbalanced, and a copy of the S335 that Gibson was making - without the refinements.

The L.P. cover of 'Freddie King Sings The Blues' - he was playing a Les Paul! I went out after seeing that cover and scoured the guitar shops and found one. That was my guitar from then on, and it sounded like Freddie King. It had everything; it was it. But Freddie's particular model, I've never seen. It looks like a Les Paul Standard but it hasn't got a sunburst top. If you check that album cover out, it's the weirdest looking beaten-up Les Paul ever.

I hear a lot of my style in other guitar players. The funny part is, the parts that I recognise as being directly taken from my playing are the parts about my playing that I don't like. Funny enough, what I like about my playing are still the parts that I copied. Like, if I'm building a solo, I'll start with a line that I know is definitely a Freddie King line, and then I'll - I'm not saying this happens consciously - go on to a BB King line. I'll do something to join them up. So that'll be me - that part. And those are the parts that I recognise when I hear something on the radio. Of course, it's not my favourite bit. My favourite bit is still the BB or Freddie lines.

Below: Cream on Ready Steady Go!, 1966.

I've always liked wah-wah, but I was scared of it for a while because it became very fashionable in the Philadelphia sound and then it sort of burned out. So I thought, "Stay clear of this for a bit." I've always liked the Hendrix wah-wah stuff, and I was in the avant-garde of that, too, with 'Tales Of Brave Ulysses'.

The only person I consider a major dobro influence is Duane Allman. He could play dobro any way, and in fact played it his way. The first dobro playing I heard that seemed to have a freedom of expression was definitely Duane's. I wasn't aware of that until we were doing the 'Layla' sessions, and there were a couple of ballads where he decided to play straight dobro. It was the only time I heard dobro that wasn't strictly confined to being country dobro - meaning lap-style dobro, very regimented. He's the only guy who played dobro free of any catalogue style. I don't have a developed style. If I were to play dobro unaccompanied I'd revert to playing like Bukka White, that kind of stuff where you're hitting the bass strings with your thumb. That's how I'd do it if I were playing a piece like 'Jitterbug Swing', one of those songs Bukka would do that had a set guitar pattern.

But if I'm playing with a band, with all the accompaniment provided, my style has to change. I normally revert to playing a melody line, and the obvious one to play on that song is the vocal line.

When I get up there on stage, I often go through a great deal of indecision, even while I'm playing. If I've got the black Stratocaster on and I'm in the middle of a blues, I'm kind of going, "Aw, I wish I had the Les Paul." Then again, if I were playing the Les Paul, the sound would be great, but I'd be going, "Man, I wish I had the Stratocaster neck." I'm always caught in the middle of those two guitars. I've always liked the Freddie King/B.B. King rich tone;

Below: Ginger Baker and Eric during Blind Faith rehearsals, February 1969.

Above: Ronnie Wood, Steve Winwood,
Eric and Ric Grech at London's Rainbow,
January 13 1973.

at the same time, I like the manic Buddy Guy/Otis Rush Strat tone.
You can get somewhere in the middle, and that's usually what I end
up doing, trying to find a happy medium. But it's bloody anguish.

All my guitars need to be ⅛" in the action, and I like it to
be constant all the way down. I can't stand it if the nut is low, and
the action gets higher as you go up the neck. I always take the wang
bar off and have five springs, and just tighten the whole thing right up.
I like frets to be generally somewhere between a Strat and a Les Paul.
Les Pauls are too thick, and Fenders are sometimes too thin.
The Fender Elite is very nice because it's a blend. The neck on
Blackie, the Strat I play all the time, is probably my favourite shape.
It's almost triangular on the back – V-shaped – with a slightly curved
fingerboard, as opposed to the flat one. That to me is best.

Blackie is made up of three different guitars. I was in Nashville
in 1970 with Derek And The Dominos and I went into the Sho-Bud
shop, and in the back they had a rack of Stratocasters and Telecasters
and various Fenders, all going for $100.00 each. No one was
playing them then. Everyone was going for Gibsons. Stevie Winwood
had kind of got me interested in them, because he was playing a
blond-necked Strat. It sounded great. Then I thought, "Well, yeah,
Buddy Guy used to play one", and I remember a great picture of

This page: The Rainbow concert.

Facing page: The American ARMS concerts,
1983. (Top) Eric, Charlie Watts and Bill
Wyman. (Below) Eric, Jimmy Page and Jeff
Beck, the three former Yardbirds guitarists
playing in public together for the first time.

Johnny Guitar Watson playing one on the 'Gangster Of Love' album.
So I just bought a handful of them and took them back to England.
I gave one to George Harrison, one to Stevie Winwood, and one to
Pete Townshend. I kept three, and out of them I made one, which is
Blackie. I just took the body from one, the neck from another, and so
on. I have no idea what the various parts are - so it's actually not a
good collector's guitar at all. Well, it is now! (laughs). I feel that that
guitar has become part of me. I get offered guitars, and endorsements
come along every now and then.

Strings & Things from Memphis tried to get me interested
in a fairly revolutionary looking guitar, the St. Blues. I tried it, and
liked it, and I played it on stage - liked it a lot. But, while I was doing
that, I was thinking, "Well, Blackie's back there. If I get into this
new guitar too deeply, it's tricky, because then I won't be able to
go back to Blackie. And what will happen to that?" This happens
in my head while I'm actually playing! I can be miles away thinking
about this stuff, and suddenly I shut down and say, "This is enough.
No more. Nice new guitar. Sorry. You're very nice, but…" That's
when I drag the old one back on, and suddenly it's just like jumping
into a pool of warm water.

There are still guitars that I want; they're like the Holy Grail
for me. There's the fat-bodied guitar that Chuck Berry played in all
the publicity photographs of him duck-walking: a Gibson ES-350.
It's got those black pick-ups. I'm always on the lookout for a good

one of those. They're actually very rare. I know of a couple, but the people won't part with them. Or if they do want to part with them, they'll quote such a high price, you say, "Well, no, that's actually silly." Because I won't play it; I only want it because it looks good. On the other hand, there will come a time when someone will walk into the dressing room with THE guitar, and you don't know why - it just is magnificent - and then you have to buy it. It could be a Les Paul, an Explorer, a Stratocaster - but it's just so perfect. You can tell that someone great has played it - you can actually tell that - then you want to take it and endow yourself with what the guitar's got.

I was never involved in pyrotechnics or gymnastics. I'm very lucky in that way. I never set myself too high a goal. It was always tone and feeling, for me. Now, sometimes I can find it difficult to reach that because you can get jaded a lot easier as you get older. A lot of the fire is gone, so you have to stop and take a breather - even when you're on stage, you can do it. But because I never went full-out for technique, I never set myself up for something too hard to keep up.

Simplicity. Roughing it up, cruding it up. That's why I like to go without playing for a while. If you're actually physically incapacitated a bit, it can make it sound nice and rough. Or you go for the more obvious things. And if you play a lot, you tend to avoid the obvious, and that's when sophistication creeps in. The last thing I want to be is sophisticated.

My guitar is still my voice. When I hear a piece of music in my head, I don't hear a song. I hear the guitar part. So I write words to that and sing it. The guitar is first and foremost in my head.

Once it's done that in my head, I use the guitar to embellish the voice. It'll always be there. I'll always try to play with the most amount of soul through the guitar. I can't do that through my voice, because I don't have that ability as a singer. I have to shift that emphasis at some point to the guitar.

Above: Eric leads an All Star Band during the ELVIS Awards, New York, 1990.

I just don't find it very inspiring to play the guitar on my own.
Playing the guitar is a very sacred experience and if I don't play on
stage or on tour I don't play at all. It's my only way of disciplining
myself. I never play at home. I don't have the necessary self control
and discipline to sit down and practise. Which is perhaps just as well
because if I did I would probably develop a style which is totally
unsuited to live music and quite alien to an improvised situation.

The thing with my technique is that I have to re-learn it over
and over again in the presence of other musicians. That's why I always
make sure the band and I have got a good long stretch of rehearsals.
Because I'm a lazy bastard and I think it's very important for me with
my personality that I walk into a rehearsal room with the least
amount to offer. I have to work twice as hard. The other guys will
come in hot from doing a session the day before and I'll be all over the
place. It's a challenge for me to climb back up again.

For the most part I can't even remember what I played the
night before, so I make it up as I go along. Mark Knopfler is a stickler
for detail and he has to play his solos exactly the same every night as
signals for the band. But I use the songs for a launch pad for going
off on a groove. The songs aren't as important to me as the grooves
I get out of them. You know how we used to do 'I Shot The Sheriff'
after 'Crossroads' and 'White Room', as the third song in every set?
Well the reason for it being there was to provide a platform for me to
gauge the audience and the band and myself, so that everyone will
know whether it's gonna be a good night or not. If it's a good solo
it's gonna be OK. If not, it'll be a struggle.

I don't dry up. Not completely, I can usually fool an audience.
I mean I can play an adequate solo any time, but what I try to do is
put myself into a state of mind where I empty myself of all ideas and
let something develop. It's like rolling the dice. You don't know what
will happen. And if it doesn't work I'll have to come back to it and

Above: Bonnie Raitt and Eric,
Wembley Stadium, 1992.

Right: Eric and Mark Knopfler at the
Royal Albert Hall, 1987.

start again in the next number, and so on all night. Because for me it's not just a case of going on and doing a show, it's got to be better than the night before, and if it's not, everyone comes off disappointed. The band always know. They give me a bollocking if I'm not pulling my weight. I wouldn't work with anyone who didn't. And that's one of the reasons I think I can sell out the Albert Hall for so many nights. Because people know it can go either way.

I play best when I'm under a lot of strain or when I think there's nothing left in me.

Eric now has his own 'Signature' series Fender Stratocaster...

Dan Smith, the guy who was head of Fender at the time, wanted to have a meeting with all the guitar players and he got all the people together in this country and kind of introduced himself which was a pretty revolutionary thing to do in a way. He came to me especially and said that he'd be very interested in putting a guitar out with my name on it and would I specify the way that I would want it.

So in actual fact, it could have been anything. If it had been someone else it probably would not have been a Stratocaster. It would have been a new shape. But when he asked me what my favourite guitar was I said 'Blackie' was it. So if they could make copies of that, especially the neck shape, I wouldn't want any changes. Just make a running list of guitars like 'Blackie', except I wanted one little thing – to fatten the sound up. To have an optional sound. So, you'd have the Stratocaster sound throughout but then you could fatten it up with just a tone knob. You've got one volume and two tones. And the second tone is this compression sound. The more you turn it clockwise, the fatter the sound gets. It's quite an individualistic sound that I like.

He asked what colours I'd like to come out in and I said "I'd like charcoal grey, Ferrari Red and 7-Up green." And that was it. I don't know if you can buy them yet, you should be able to.

It's exactly the same as 'Blackie'. So, I think that anyone who buys one will be very happy with it. This is the most satisfying guitar for me to play. (1988)

'Blackie' is his all-time favourite Fender Strat...

It's at home. It's off the road completely. I play it at home occasionally, but it's too precious for me to take out for fear of loss or breakage or something like that. But, the great thing about this new guitar is that it's brand new, the same as 'Blackie' is old, if you know what I mean. All the years it took to get 'Blackie' the way it was, you can buy in a store now, brand new. So that's a bonus. (1988)

Eric Clapton and Friends

The Bunburys

The first single was 'We Are The Bunburys' by The Bunburys, who at the time were The Bee Gees. David English invented the Bunburys as a cartoon and he put out the books first of all. They were illustrated by a guy called Jan Brychta, and David English would write the story. And then he thought about making music to go with it. He's an old friend of Barry Gibb's. Those two started writing and Barry wrote a song for me to do which hasn't been released yet, called 'Fight', and will be out on The Bunburys' album. Elton's on it and George Harrison is on it. It's been held up for one reason or another because I don't know what label it's coming out on yet. But it's good stuff and I think it's going to be an ongoing thing for David. (1988)

Robert Cray

I think the world of Robert Cray. I just heard his new album ('Don't Be Afraid Of The Dark'), I don't think it's out yet, and it's phenomenal. It's better than ever. He just improves.

Duck Dunn played me a cassette of him many years ago. About five years ago I first heard whatever album it is that 'Bad Influence' is on, and thought it was fantastic. The first time I saw him live was at the Montreux Jazz Festival in 1986. I sat and watched his set and I was just freaked out. And the funny thing was that his bass player, who is a bit of a wag, said at the end of their set, "How about a round of applause for Robert Cray. Sixteen years old, genius!" And I believed it! (1988)

Facing page: Lionel Richie and Eric in New York, 1986.

Below: Buddy Guy, Robert Cray, Jimmie Vaughan and Eric during a Royal Albert Hall Blues Night, 1991.

Bruce Springsteen

He's fabulous. I can't believe that man. And I haven't seen the
show yet. I'm actually frightened to go see it now. I've heard so much.
You know, it's like when someone tells you how funny a joke is,
then you hear the joke and it isn't funny. But I know that isn't going
to happen with him. I'm so much in awe of him I'll probably retire
after seeing his show. (1985)

Prince

He's great. I went to the film opening of 'Purple Rain', and it
tore my head off. I just loved it, really did love it. I went back to the
UK screaming about how wonderful he was; I played the record for
everyone and tried to get hold of a video. I was just completely
converted.

   Then he came to England and they hated him. They slaughtered
him, because he came over the way he his - he and his bodyguard, it
was very much a showbiz-type trip - and the English people couldn't
take it. If you're a pop star you have to be a good after-dinner
speaker. And he just didn't fit in. But to me, he's what rock'n'roll's
all about.

   I jammed with him once on 'Can't Get Next To You', an
old Al Green song, for about half an hour. It was fantastic, it was
like three or four blues tunes. And when I walked into the club, his
manager was trying to wind me up saying, "Go on, just walk up there
and pat him on the shoulder and say something witty," you know.
And I couldn't do it. I just didn't have the bottle because I'd never
met Prince.

   Prince saw me and invited me up in the end. And it was great!
I mean, he was such a nice guy, so polite. And so humble. I expected
it actually, because my experience says that if a musician is good
musically, usually they are really nice people too. Music never lies
really. That's the way he was, and such a great player. He played
everything that night, bass, drums, keyboards, guitar, so much energy.
And he'd just played two hours at Wembley.

   I was going to play with him again a couple of years later at the
Camden Palace. I was pretty tired when I arrived as I'd just finished
working with Mickey Rourke on his film Homeboy. We worked
'til late and we went to see Prince afterwards and he came and
introduced himself. He walked around the club and introduced
himself to everybody in there, which is pretty unexpected for him
because he's so shy. And he said he'd like me to play. I said,
"When you want me to play, just call me up," and I waited for
about an hour and a half. It was about four in the morning by then
and I was bushed, so I went home. (1988)

George Harrison

We're very different, because he has a very strong sense of rejection of the material world, whereas I want to face it and fight it, but musically we are kindred spirits. That's what joins us together, because he loves what I do, and he can't do it, while I love what he does, but I can't do it. I mean there's no way I could play the slide the way he does: he's fantastic, the first man who had the idea of playing a melody, instead of just trying to play like Elmore James. He's achieved that, and just doing that is enough.

In 1991 Eric was instrumental in persuading Harrison to make a short tour of Japan...

It's certainly not for business. I've been concerned about George. I love touring, it's my favourite experience and I keep telling him that, yet his response is a cynical "Really?" He can't believe it because 15 years without touring is a long time. And all the experience he had in his early days with The Beatles was bizarre because they were playing for 10-year-olds through a set of, say, 40 minutes, knowing no one could hear them, then hop into a helicopter and be gone. And then when he did a solo tour 15 years ago he lost his voice on the first night! That left him determined never to do it again. So those are the barriers we have to break down and I hope we do.

The whole idea is that George should go, with my band, and perform songs that he's been famous for nearly 30 years, from the time of The Beatles onwards. And despite working with The Wilburys he considers himself retired from the music business because he's so disillusioned with it all. But I told him that everywhere I played last year people were asking, "Where's George Harrison? What is he doing?" and we started talking about doing some shows together. He was very nervous, so I said, "You can have my band, my lights, my sound and we'll go somewhere where people are not too critical and are hungry and enthusiastic - like Japan." So if that works, if he enjoys it, maybe we will do Europe and America.

Above: George Harrison and Eric at Wembley Arena, June 1987.

Below: George and Eric at JFK Airport, New York, 1989.

There are so many great songs. We could do the whole of 'All Things Must Pass' for a start but every album's got some great songs. It will be interesting to see if we can play that stuff because they're pop songs. Steve Ferrone, my drummer, doesn't know how to play any way but loud and I'm always inclined to slip into a groove.

George is very paranoid about the press. There's a lot of anger in him. I don't know why. He's got his guard up before he begins. But the worst they can say is that he's a boring old fart. And that's almost gone out of fashion. (1991)

Eddie Van Halen

Eddie's great. I'm not really mad about the band. I think his technique is probably just a little too frenetic sometimes, but his idea of tone is correct, if you like. It's just a question of time before he really does become, you know, the greatest. (1985)

Mark Knopfler

Below: Mark Knopfler and Eric during Eric's 1988 US tour.

Well, Mark Knopfler, I think, is totally unique. He's a great craftsman, which brings it back to that. I mean, within Dire Straits, if you listen to

any of their albums the first time, it sort of goes by you a bit, and then gradually it just gets better and better, and it stands the test of time. They're fantastic craftsmen. (1988)

Eric played at Chuck Berry's 60th Birthday Concert...

The first thing that happened is when I arrived, I went to the hotel and could have gone straight to bed, having just got off the plane. But I thought I would go down to rehearsals and see what was happening. It was pretty late, about eleven o'clock at night, and everyone was there except Chuck. I didn't see him anywhere, and asked where he was and someone said "I'll go get him."

Chuck appeared and he sat down next to me on the couch and he said, "Hi, I'm Chuck Berry, you're Eric Clapton. Nice to meet you." Then he said, "Hang on a second!" and shouted out "Bring the camera in!"

So next thing I knew, this person holding a camera and microphone walked into the situation. Then Chuck turned to me and said, "Okay, so when was it you really got into my music?!" He started interviewing me about himself, and before the interview was over, I was interviewing him about himself.

I still love his music, but meeting him in some senses took the edge off it for me. I found out bit by bit that he was so concerned with money and himself, and he is such an ambitious man, that in a way kind of spoiled the feeling for the music.

He's a very dark horse. He definitely does have that feeling that people ripped him off and stole all his licks.

He's very shrewd. He's got his fingers in all sorts of pies. At the rehearsals people would be wanting to borrow an amp and they'd find they were hiring it from him! But I sort of admire that kind of thing. It's slightly Irish in a way. (1988)

Jimi Hendrix

He got up and played two songs with us (Cream) and I knew it was all over in terms of guitar heroes. Jimi had everything. He'd got all the tricks, he played like a genius but he could also play it with his teeth or behind his head or on the ground. Jack and Ginger did not like it at all. They probably saw the end of their careers looming. He was going to get a trio and tour, just like us.

I didn't see Hendrix in terms of competition. I just thought; a kindred spirit! Someone I can talk to about the music I love. We just fell in love with one another but everybody else was very: Who's this? Can't have this round here.

Reaching 40: A Gentleman's Pursuits

I'm very relieved. Thank God I got here. There was a time there when I didn't think I'd make it. I hated my 30's. I enjoyed my 20's, although I was a very serious person then. In my 30's I just dissipated, and by the time I was 33 I was really unsure of what I was here for. Now that I've reached 40 I can relax, in a way.

(Fishing) is very absorbing, and the ideal pursuit for someone who wants a solitary activity. It's a good time to think about everything and get it in perspective. I get a lot of good thinking done when I'm fishing.

My obsession is dry fly fishing. You have to have pretty good conditions to do it in. Not bright sunshine, but not rain either, and it's one of the things, you know, I don't get enough time to do it.

Four or five years ago, I was fishing nearly every day. And I'd like to get back to a happy medium. I mean a happy medium would be to be able to fish at least once a week or twice a week sometimes.

I grew up in Ripley which is supposed to have the biggest village green in the country. So I used to watch a great deal of cricket. Most of my childhood idols were cricketers and sportsmen of the village. You know, small scale – but when you are a little boy these things have a great deal of importance.

Then I suppose I was always interested in the Test Match scores right through my life. But it's just like fishing. It's one of those things you can return to when your life starts to slow down a bit and you get time to relax.

Right: Eric fails to get to the pitch of the ball and an in swinger demolishes his off stump, much to the delight of wicket-keeper David Capel (England and Northants).

My ideal fantasy of England when I'm away from home is
going to Lord's and watching cricket or being by the river Test with
a fly rod. Those are the things that sum up England for me more than
anything. The fact that it rarely happens because of the weather is
another matter.

I have been collecting Ferraris for the last twenty years. I must have
had about twenty of his cars in that time. I have three at the moment
(1988) and I'm trying to acquire another one right now because there
were a couple of cars that he made which I thought were always pretty
overlooked as being collectors' items. One of them has just become

available and I thought it would be nice to have it. If you look at it as a business investment, it is probably more profitable than property.

I was mad about clothes in The Yardbirds and I was trying to get the others interested too, but that was a waste of time. I was just mad about Ivy League then, and there was one shop in Piccadilly that sold imported American suits - especially modern Ivy League suits, the ones with one button. It was unbelievably difficult to find this stuff, and you'd pay through the nose for it. No one else was wearing it.

It was like the beginning of the mod period, and not long after that everyone had crewcuts and was riding scooters and wearing anoraks. I guess I could have been a fashion designer or gotten into that world because I've always been fascinated by clothes. One of the reasons I think I was edged out of The Yardbirds was because, having had long hair - and they were all just developing Beatle-style haircuts - I went and got myself a crewcut. That shook everybody up! Whoa, they could not handle that at all.

I always used to buy jazz albums on Blue Note, and even when I was just buying blues albums I'd go into the record shops and flip through the bins and pick out something by Miles Davis, and see this guy impeccably dressed. The way these guys presented themselves attracted me to the jazz world much more than the music. They were sharp. And people like Ray Charles would go to a session wearing a shirt and tie and a suit. Guys now wear track suits! (laughter) I mean, what's it all about?!

I've always loved clothes. I remember buying my first suit out of a second-hand shop in Richmond. It was a pin-stripe and I had it altered to make it really natty so that I could go to the Hammersmith Palais and hang out with the mods.

My clothes are all Italian usually. If I'm not wearing Levis and a t-shirt, then I buy all my clothes from an Italian designer in Bond Street. It goes in waves. Sometimes, I go on a spending spree that lasts for days and other times clothes don't bother me at all. It comes and goes.

I've got a large collection going back over the last ten years. Every now and then I weed it out and Cranleigh Oxfam get a nice slice of Armani.

I have always liked beautiful things, be it clothes, jewellery, cars, paintings, women (laughs) and music. I learned quite early on that you don't have to own something to admire it as it is. But in terms of presenting myself, I have always wanted to be able to look as good as I could. That is why I have always changed my appearance. I did go through a period where I was obsessed by clothes, but I am not in that frame of mind any more. Now I wear just what I feel like. That is not to say that I won't change my mind next year.

Women and Marriage

The groupie scene in America was red hot. I first went there to do a Murray The K show with The Who and there were tons of them around then. I mean, pretty ugly ones but some fair ones too. There were both ends really - horrible little scrubbers and really nice looking middle class chicks. Or just nice chicks who didn't realise they were making themselves into groupies - they were pretty innocent.

There are some chicks around who really are fucked-up in their heads and as a result they probably were carrying on like that at the time, but afterwards they feel so ashamed that they can't lead a straight life with anyone. They probably think they're whores. But as a rule they're the most incredibly warm people. I mean, there are a few exceptions - chicks who are just out to be superstar groupies because it's become the thing to do, but in the early days they were just chicks who wanted to look after you when you were in town. If making love to you was going to make you happy, they'd make love. If you were tired and didn't want to make it, they'd cook you a meal and make you feel at home. They really were 'ports of call'.

I think I've laid over a thousand girls now. It was a childhood ambition. Well, I thought I'd missed out a great deal because I didn't know about the facts of life 'til I was nine and I thought everyone else had known them ever since they came out the womb. So I thought I'd really missed out. I thought things were going on all around me that I didn't know about and I made up my mind to do something about it. In fact I don't think that was the case at all. I don't think anyone knows that much about it until they're nine, ten or eleven, and some people don't know about it until they're fifty or something.

I love doing anything with women. I prefer the company of women to men. When I meet a female I get on very well with, something creative seems to take place. With another man, I find it difficult sometimes, because if a man is a capable songwriter, he's usually got a drive or an ambition that will keep me reticent. And I will let that ride roughshod over me.

With a woman, when you're writing, they don't have that edge. They're much more giving. That's just the way women are, or they were. I mean, things have changed! You're running into a whole different woman these days. There's now a lot of masculinity amongst the female gender. The whole thing of being independent and a working woman has taken a lot out of it.

The only thing that meant anything to me was 'Layla', which
was because it was actually about an emotional experience, a woman
(Patti Harrison) that I felt really deeply about and that turned me
down, and I had to kind of pour it out in some way. So we wrote
these songs, made an album, and the whole thing was great.
She didn't give a damn.

I remember George (Harrison) saying something like "Better she's
with some drunken Yardbird than some old dope", or something like
that. Yeah, I still get on with George. Still, we have our little bickers
now and then. But I've known him too long not to still love him.
I've known George since we were kids… and we both had that
fire that we'll try the rest of our lives to preserve.

George put both mine and Patti's names on the credits for 'Bye
Bye Love' on his 'Dark Horse' album. I can't remember what he said,
but everyone took it to mean we're playing on it. In actual fact, he
did the whole thing on his own. He sent me the tapes just after he'd
done it. He played everything on it.

Patti was getting ready to go out. We were about two hours late.
I was furious. 'Cause I hate unpunctuality. I'm very punctual myself
and can't tolerate it in other people. She was always late. I was sitting
downstairs, and I'd been ready for two hours. I went upstairs to see
what was going on, and she was up there with one of her girlfriends,
still trying on different things. I said, "Well that's nice - what is it,
a curtain? You look wonderful!"

    I went back downstairs and while I was waiting I picked up the
guitar and I started writing that song ('Wonderful Tonight'). It wasn't
in the sense of love or affection. It was written just to pass the time,
and I was pretty angry.

    That lady can draw a lot out of people. She has that ability.

Above: Patti Boyd and Eric backstage at
Live Aid in Philadelphia, July 1985.

Facing page:
Ozzy Osbourne, Grace Jones and Eric
in 1989.

We had our separation as a sort of mutual agreement. It was something that we both discussed amongst ourselves as two people. But you forget that other people are interested in what you're doing. And when it got into the papers – the way they wrote about it – it really did hurt, because it hadn't occurred to me up until that point that it was really anyone else's business. And when you see it all in black and white it tends to become almost a little too real. You start believing what you read, and it multiplies the grief of all of it.

Below: Lory Del Santo with Eric's baby son, Conor.

As far as what happened with us, the problem was on both
sides. Well, I probably – definitely – instigated it in many areas.
First by not involving her in my musical life. I tend to get very
wrapped up in things. And this was happening during the period that
I stopped drinking, and I was very dogmatic about that. You see, she
likes to drink and I became very strict about that and I started to put
her down. I was very intolerant. Then I would go out on the road and
not take her with me; and so we began to drift apart. And after about
a year of that you come to the realisation that you've got very little
in common any more. And that's when we decided to sit down and
look at our marriage, and decided to have a trial separation.
And thank God we found out during that time that there was a
fairly strong bond there that we hadn't considered at all. Neither of
us had really understood this, but there's a real thread that holds us
together. In actual fact, it was a good thing for us to have split,
because we had a chance to find out how much we really did miss
one another.

It was best that we got divorced. With the birth of my son Conor it
was impossible for Patti. I would have liked, I mean, I probably would
have struggled to keep the whole thing going, juggling like crazy
but it would have driven someone mad, and probably me.

Above: Eric and Lory.

Right: Conor and Lory.

Drugs, Alcohol and Death

The first time I took acid was when we did the cover for 'Disraeli Gears' and we went up to Scotland and we took it at the bottom of Ben Nevis and then went up to the top. It was amazing. We ran down! Have you ever tried running down a mountain? You see, Ben Nevis is not steep because you've got this spiral path which goes all the way to the top and it's about a five mile walk. It took us about half a day to get to the top and then three hours to run down. You know, it was the kind of running where you can't stop... you've just got to make the best of it. Incredible feeling. As a matter of fact I didn't trip that much; I only ever had one bad trip and it wasn't extremely bad – I just thought I was going to die. But, I mean, it was all right because I thought, well, if I'm going to die it doesn't matter. I'll just go and lie somewhere. So I went into a room, lay down on a bed and waited to die. I can remember people coming in and saying, "Are you all right?" and me saying, "Oh yes. Leave me alone. I'm dying." It wasn't that bad at the time. it was just the expectation of dying.

The thing about acid is that you've really got to put all your trust in it because you don't know where you're going to come down after a trip. I mean, you can come down in a weird place where you don't want to be and never be able to get out again.

When recording the 'Layla' album in Florida, we were very fit. We would have saunas, go swimming during the day and then go to the studio and get loaded. It didn't affect the playing or the sessions. But as is the way with drugs, it would catch up later.

We scored a massive amount of coke and H (heroin) before we left Florida and took it on tour. I don't know how we got through it with the amount we were taking. I couldn't do it now; I would die now. Even the idea frightens me. But it definitely wore the band down and introduced a lot of hostility that wasn't naturally there. It drove a wedge between each one of us.

By the time of the second Dominos' album sessions, money and dope and women were getting so far involved with our nucleus that we couldn't communicate any more. I remember it came to a crunch when one day Jim (Gordon) was playing drums, and he heard that I'd made some remark about a drummer in another band. I don't remember making the remark, but he got up from behind the kit and said, "Why don't you get so-and-so in here? He could play

it better than I could!" and walked out. And we never went back to
the studio again. It was that dramatic.

There was a real feeling of sadness there, of futility. The tapes
stayed in the studio. I never went back. Nor did the others.

I went back home and stayed there and locked all the doors.

I've been drinking hard since I was fifteen. It's a pretty vicious circle.
Vicious? No, it's quite nice really! I went from drinking to taking pills
to taking something else. There's always some kind of buzz going on.
I don't think I've spent more than a week of my life when I haven't
been tampering around with something.

In America they knew who I was at AA meetings. I went to one
in St Paul where I'd played a concert the night before and everyone
had Eric Clapton T-shirts on. A couple of the younger ones got very
emotional about me being there. One girl had a real breakdown,
crying and apologising to me, saying she'd been to the concert the
night before and said to her friend, I bet he's in the dressing room
drinking and tooting coke. But in England you're dealing more with
the tweeds and the brigadiers. Anyone under 50 they don't take
seriously anyway.

I was a practising alcoholic when I made the remake of 'After
Midnight' for a Michelob beer commercial. By the time it came
out I was in treatment. This was December of '87. I was actually in
treatment in Minnesota when that came on TV. I was in a room
full of recovering alcoholics, myself being one of them, and everybody
went, "Is that you?" I said, "Yep." What was I going to say? It was
me when I was drinking.

Below: Eric, David Letterman, Phil Collins
and Paul Schaffer, the band leader from the
Letterman show. 1985.

I don't know if it was offered to me now whether I would do it. But then again, I'm not a preacher. I'm not one to say whether people should be drinking or not. Otherwise, I'd have to come down hard on all my mates, like Phil (Collins), who does it as well. I can only speak for myself. I don't drink any more, and I'd rather not drink ever again.

The first shock came when I had to go to an airport and get on a plane and then check into a hotel and I didn't know how to do it. I thought I've taken so many flights and I don't even know the first step in how to get on an aeroplane. When a guy 35 years old doesn't know how to do that it's pretty bad.

The last five years have been a very accelerated acceptance of my responsibility. I don't think anything's improved a great deal. I'm still not very sure of myself away from music.

Death...

Bobby Brooks, my agent, was in the helicopter with Stevie Ray (Vaughan), as were Nigel Browne and Colin Smythe of my crew.

There was a convoy of helicopters, about five of them, and they had to go back through this very thick fog up to about 100 feet above the ground. And once we came out of that, we just took off for Chicago. And when I got back, I went straight to bed. And I was woken about seven in the morning by my manager, Roger Forrester, saying that the helicopter with Stevie Ray and our chaps hadn't come back. And then a bit later, someone discovered the wreckage. That was it.

Right: Stevie Ray Vaughan.

I had a meeting with all the bands and the managers. And all
the crew had gone to the next show, so we got them on the phone,
and we tried to come up with a unanimous decision about whether we
should go home or whether we should go on. And the vote came out,
after hours of discussion, that we should carry on. It was clearly felt
that if we packed up and went home, the whole thing would just be
unbearable. So we went to… I think it was St. Louis, or somewhere in
the Midwest, and we were almost in shock. I could hardly remember
any of the words. I don't know how we got through it. But it was the
best tribute I thought we could make – to carry on and let everybody
who was coming to see us know it was in honour of their memory.

    The worst thing for me was that Stevie Ray had been sober
for three years and was at his peak. When he played that night, he had
all of us standing there with our jaws dropped. I mean, Robert Cray
and Jimmie Vaughan and Buddy Guy were just in awe. There was
no one better than him on this planet. Really unbelievable. (1991)

After my son died, all kinds of people turned up for different
reasons.

    There is a kind of woman I think that sees it as a fantastic
opportunity for either gain or, maybe, even to give me something.
I had letters from women who wanted to be surrogate wives with
families. I had letters from women who said I have got a girl who is
four and we would love to move in with you and help you start
your life again.

    I started writing right after he died but I couldn't really put into
words what I was feeling because I didn't want it to be trite. I didn't
really want anyone to know and I didn't want to know myself. I didn't
want to hear what I had to say and it took a long time.

Above: Steve Ray Vaughan's last show at
Alpine Valley Music Theatre, August 26, 1990,
left to right: Stevie, Phil Palmer, Ray Cooper,
Jimmy Vaughan, Buddy Guy and Eric.

Above and below: Conor Clapton in 1989.

I think I was as close as I have ever been to anybody. It was probably the closest relationship I have ever had because I invested so much hope into it. Ironically, this was to be the year that I would stop working altogether for a while so that we could specifically spend more time together.

It was a big challenge for me to try to put my life in order so I could make my son's life more settled. And it was getting to the point - before he died - where we could really look at raising my son in some kind of balanced way.

We tried to live together as a family a couple of times, but I think my inability to settle down - which is something I'm still working on - prevented that from ever happening. It seems to be almost impossible for me to find myself in a relationship without wanting to get away at some point, wanting to run away and go and be a little boy again and play the guitar and misbehave. I don't know whether I'll ever grow up, but I mean, it seems to be my goal now, to try to grow up gradually without losing the things that I enjoy in life.

I wonder, "Why me? Why have I survived?" I have to look at that as the positive. I have survived these things, and therefore I've got some kind of responsibility to remain positively creative and not dwell on the misfortune of it.

The death of my son and Stevie Ray taught me that life is very fragile, and that if you are given another twenty-four hours, it's a blessing. That's the best way to look at it.

Eric by his Peers

Tom McGuinness

I'd love to be able to say that the minute Eric picked up a guitar
I knew he was a genius, but that just wasn't the case at that time.
We both played lead guitar and I didn't feel intimidated for one
minute. Of course, I did a couple of years later, when he got into
The Bluesbreakers. Then he was really, really good. But in The
Roosters we were just a couple of kids who loved the blues. I never
felt that I was in the presence of someone who would turn out to be
as good as Eric Clapton.

Jeff Beck

I really take a whole different view on Eric now because I've managed
to get myself into a position where I can enjoy his playing. He no
longer has anything to do with my style - you know, at one time we
were both blues. And he was better. I think he can play blues better
than I can because he studies and is loyal to it.

Below: Jimmy Page, Eric and Jeff Beck
during the ARMS tour, 1983.

John Mayall

I saw Eric very early on with The Yardbirds a couple of times
but at that time he hadn't really gotten his chops together. But I did
think he was the only one in the band that was any use at all – to
my ears anyway. Eric was the only one I'd heard in England who had
any of what the blues was all about. The others didn't have what
Eric had – but then, nobody has what Eric had.

He blossomed very rapidly when he joined my band. In the
course of the year that he was with me, he made very remarkable
strides. He was a very moody player… by that I mean he'd conjure up
these incredible moods and intensity. The things he did with a slow
blues could send shivers down your spine. With my band Eric became
the way to play, so anybody who followed him was going to be
automatically compared with Eric. That's a very tough act to follow.

Mike Bloomfield

Clapton – I thought, now here's a guy, here's a rock star.
Boy, did he play. I thought… if only I could do what he could do.
I thought he had taken the blues just absolutely as far as it could go.

Gregg Allman

I think 'Layla' was probably my brother Duane's favourite session…

Right: Phil Collins and Eric, 1985.

Elton John

Eric Clapton could come out in a dress and I wouldn't mind, as long
as he was carrying his guitar.

John Williams

Eric Clapton is a great god of mine. It doesn't matter whether
he's playing a fantastic song or a slightly boring one, or whether he
was better at the concert he gave two years ago or the one he gave
last week - all that is immaterial because, basically, the guy is a genius
with a wonderful style of playing and feel for the instrument.

Brian May

I was impressed by Clapton from the very beginning, because
I used to go and see The Yardbirds. We did a couple of their songs.
Clapton was unbelievable, just so sparkling and fluid. He was what
turned me away from the Shadows style and sent me back to listening
to B. B. King, Bo Diddley and all those people. I didn't realise the
depth or emotion there was in the music until I saw Eric Clapton.
That somehow made it accessible for me.

Above: Eric with Elton John in 1992.

Coda

I think that was very shrewd on my part to choose a role that I could be fulfilling at the age of 60. I was reading where Sting said that he was going into films because he didn't want to be like Mick Jagger, cavorting around the stage at 40. Well, I've never done that, so I don't have to worry. I can do what I've been doing all my life.

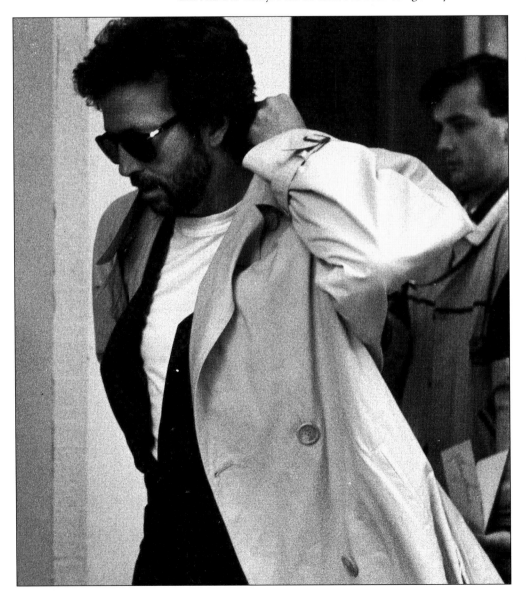